Text © 2006 by Monte Farber
Art © 2006 by Amy Zerner

10 9 8 7 6 5 4 3 2

Published by Sterling Publishing Co., Inc.
387 Park Avenue South, New York, NY 10016

Distributed in Canada by Sterling Publishing
c/o Canadian Manda Group, 165 Dufferin Street
Toronto, Ontario, Canada M6K 3H6

Distributed in the United Kingdom by GMC
Distribution Services
Castle Place, 166 High Street, Lewes, East Sussex,
England BN7 1XU

Distributed in Australia by Capricorn Link (Australia)
Pty. Ltd.
P.O. Box 704, Windsor, NSW 2756, Australia

Printed in China

Sterling ISBN-13: 978-1-4027-4179-1
        ISBN-10: 1-4027-4179-0

For information about custom editions, special sales,
premium and corporate purchases, please contact
Sterling Special Sales Department at 800-805-5489 or
specialsales@sterlingpub.com.

# What's Your Sign?

When someone asks you "What's your sign?" you know what that person really means is "What's your astrological sign?" Professional astrologers more often use the phrase "Sun sign," a term reflecting the concept that a person's sign is determined by which of the twelve signs of the zodiac the Sun appeared to be passing through at the moment she was born. The zodiac is the narrow band of sky circling the Earth's equator through which the Sun, the Moon, and the planets appear to move when viewed by us here on Earth.

# Astrology's Gift

Astrology, which has been around for thousands of years, is the study of how planetary positions relate to earthly events and people. Its long and rich history has resulted in a wealth of philosophical and psychological wisdom, the basic concepts of which we are going to share with you in the pages of this book. As the Greek philosopher Heracleitus (c. 540–c. 480 BCE) said, "Character is destiny." Who you are—complete with all of your goals, tendencies, habits, virtues, and vices—will

determine how you act and react, thereby creating your life's destiny. Like astrology itself, our Astrology Gems series is designed to help you to better know yourself and those you care about. You will then be better able to use your free will to shape your life to your liking.

# Does Astrology Work?

Many people rightly question how astrology can divide humanity into twelve Sun signs and make predictions that can be correct for everyone of the same sign. The simple answer is that it cannot do that—that's newspaper astrology, entertaining but not the real thing. Rather, astrology can help you understand your strengths and weaknesses so that you can better accept yourself as you are and use your strengths to compensate for your weaknesses. Real astrology is designed to help you to become yourself fully.

Remember, virtually all the music in the history of Western music has been composed using variations of the same twelve notes. Similarly, the twelve Sun signs of astrology are basic themes rich with meaning that each of us expresses differently to create and respond to the unique opportunities and challenges of our life.

# GEMINI

## May 21–June 20

**Planet**
Mercury

**Element**
Air

**Quality**
Mutable

**Day**
Wednesday

**Season**
summer

**Colors**
white, yellow

# Plants
sweet pea, lily of the valley, mint

# Perfume
lavender

# Gemstones
quartz crystal, tiger's eye, topaz,
bicolored tourmaline

# Metal
quicksilver

# Personal qualities
Witty, changeable, versatile,
talkative, well read

## KEYWORDS

We call the following words "keywords" because they can help you unlock the core meaning of the astrological sign of Gemini. Each keyword represents issues and ideas that are of supreme importance and prominence in the lives of people born with Gemini as their Sun sign. You will usually find that every Gemini embodies at least one of these keywords in the way she makes a living:

haste · logic · social skills
communication · mischief
restlessness · gossip · versatility
precocity · life of the mind
rumor mill · advertising
adaptability · talkative · curiosity
salesmanship · travel · the media
quick wit · numbers · estimate
sound bites · information

# Gemini's Symbolic Meaning

Thousands of years ago, the ancient sages were wise to pick as the symbol for Gemini a pair of twins. For it is as if there exist within the Gemini two different people with two different sets of values and opinions. Personifying this concept of duality, Geminis are known for functioning best when they have two or more things to do at the same time.

Those born under the sign of the Twins are among the best communicators of information, in terms of both relaying what they've learned and expressing their opinions. However, though they speak clearly, their tendency to use big words and long sentences often results in others having difficulty understanding the precise nature of what Geminis are trying to say.

Interested in everything, Geminis become skilled at anything they put their lightning-quick minds to. They are also the most versatile of signs: It is rare for a Gemini to do only one thing extremely well. Additionally, those born under this sign have great mental dexterity. Their desire to comprehend and communicate quickly produces both an endless curiosity and an ability to take every side of an issue.

Gemini is one of the four Mutable, or changeable, signs of the zodiac. (The other three are Sagittarius, Pisces, and Virgo.) Mutable signs are flexible and variable—they know how to adapt and adjust. Geminis are curious to know everything there is to know, and they are more than willing to adjust their beliefs when information that appeals to them comes along. All Mutable signs possess a talent for duality, but because Gemini is the sign of the Twins, this trait is strongest in them.

Gemini has an abundance of intellectual energy, which ties in to its being one of the three Air signs (the other two are Aquarius and Libra). Air signs have in common the desire for communication and freedom of expression, thought, and movement. Air is a metaphor for the invisible thoughts and ideas that motivate Gemini.

Geminis love to gossip. While most don't engage in this activity more than other people, they are better at it and delight in it more. You can bet that when a Gemini tells you something, it is the most up-to-date information available. Geminis love to be up on the latest things, and they try their best to know something about everything. Their curiosity is legendary. Geminis think that if they only had the time and access to enough information, they could actually come to know everything.

## Recognizing a Gemini

Geminis can be tall and usually have long arms and legs. While highly agile and light on their feet, they can be somewhat clumsy when hurrying. Possessing a great deal of nervous energy, they find it difficult to sit still, and they tend to use their hands to express themselves. They generally smile and laugh a lot, and have a knack for looking younger than they really are.

## Gemini's Typical Behavior and Personality Traits

- friendly and outgoing
- intelligent and witty
- graced with superior social skills
- expert at telling jokes and stories
- gives useful advice
- optimistic and upbeat
- takes an interest in friends' interests

- loves to read
- curious about many subjects
- adept at multitasking
- may change his mind often

# What Makes a Gemini Tick?

Geminis want to experience life fully and in as many different ways as they can. They may even go so far as to live something of a double life. At the very least, they have two opinions about everything—more, if they have actually studied a particular subject in depth. Geminis hunger for information from all sources: books, television, word of mouth. They will do practically anything to avoid being bored—which, to a Gemini, is a fate almost worse than death.

# The Gemini
# Personality
# Expressed Positively

Geminis who are interested in everything are expressing the best qualities of their sign: versatility, dexterity, and intelligence. When Geminis are happy they are a joy to be around, displaying their intelligence in a witty way that isn't snobbish or vain. And they delight in being able to help anyone who is not as quick-witted, knowledgeable, or versatile as they are.

## On a Positive Note

*Geminis displaying the positive characteristics associated with their sign also tend to be:*

- 🌸 articulate and entertaining
- 🌸 adaptable and versatile
- 🌸 open to alternative ways of thinking
- 🌸 good with their hands
- 🌸 youthful in attitude and appearance
- 🌸 witty and charming
- 🌸 inquisitive and smart
- 🌸 graced with a quick mind and body
- 🌸 intuitive

# The Gemini Personality Expressed Negatively

Few people who see the lighthearted and upbeat side of Gemini ever suspect that the very same person can often feel desperately alone and lost. This is usually caused by the Gemini's tendency to distance herself from her feelings and examine them as if they belong to someone else. If a Gemini doesn't have a way to channel her love and need for communication, there is a tendency to turn sarcastic and critical.

## Negative Traits

*Geminis displaying the negative characteristics associated with their sign also tend to be:*

* prone to boredom
* often nervous and restless
* fickle and unreliable
* impatient and irritable
* impractical with money
* gossipy and likely to tell fibs
* quick to size people up
* untrue to their word

# Ask a Gemini If...

Ask a Gemini if you want to know how to get to a specific location. Those born under the sign of the Twins have a flawless sense of direction and will probably also treat you to a history of the place, as well as other background information. You can also depend on them for the details of what is going on in the world, because no matter how demanding their schedules may be, Geminis always manage to read the paper or catch the news on television or online.

# Geminis As Friends

Geminis make for spirited, fun friends who are eager to try new adventures. Drawn to lively, intelligent conversations, they like people who share their curiosity about the world. They generally enjoy spending time with individuals who respond well to or enjoy spontaneous activities and spur-of-the-moment plans. Geminis never want to miss anything, and hence may end up being early or late for a get-together. They love to network and are not at all possessive when it comes to sharing their contacts.

Geminis will keep friends amused with endless observations, stories, bits of information, or the latest gossip. Often the friendships won't last long because the restless and fickle Gemini nature gets bored quickly and thus is always ready to move on, meet new people, and make new friends.

# Looking for Love

Geminis may sometimes find that they are interested in more than one person, even if they are in a committed relationship. It is also possible that more than one person may be interested in them. There can be quite a difference in age, station in life, or educational background between a Gemini and her partner(s), because those born under the sign of the Twins see variety as the spice of life, something to be savored and enjoyed. Rather than look for carbon copies of themselves, Geminis are challenged and excited by intellectual, emotional, and spiritual differences. Because of their adaptable nature, they find it easy to embrace the interests and hobbies of others.

Reading, writing, learning, and growing must be an important part of any new relationship a Gemini enters. Taking courses or developing skills together can improve the chances of love blossoming. For a Gemini, the promise of an intellectual partnership may be what is most attractive in another individual. It is practically impossible for Geminis to be romantic with someone with whom they can't communicate.

Jealousy may enter the picture because the Gemini is not home or is paying a lot of attention to others around him. This may appear to be flightiness, but it is a way of being honest to the sign's nature. Geminis like to relate to many people at the same time—otherwise, they might get bored. It can be difficult for Geminis to make peace with the idea that one person can satisfy all of their needs. But even if they can come to grips with the concept of sexual fidelity, the typical Gemini may still have to go to one or more other partners for intellectual or emotional stimulation.

# Finding That Special Someone

Geminis love to flirt, and it can be difficult to spot someone special amongst their many crushes. Finding a special someone frightens Geminis out of superficiality, and they must avoid becoming overly serious and obsessive in their effort to keep this special person around. Geminis need stimulating communication. They are likely to meet romantic partners in places where they can feel secure, such as in Internet chat rooms, bookstores, libraries, and museums. Anything related to learning and scholarship, including debates, will put them in the mood.

# First Dates

The perfect first date should take place in a conversation-friendly zone. Given Gemini's love of being up on the latest and greatest, a unique or trendy restaurant makes for an appropriate setting. Food isn't really a Gemini "thing," but when it comes to eateries, ambience matters a great deal. Going to the movies, especially to see a comedy, is always a great first date for Gemini, so long as there is the opportunity to go somewhere afterward and talk about it. The same holds true for a motivational lecture, seminar, play, or other cultural activity.

# Gemini in Love

Geminis seek variety in love and enjoy surprises and lighthearted romance. Geminis want friendship, warmth, and shared ideas. They enjoy humor in a relationship, but they prize communication. They have great instincts about people and rarely jump into a relationship without first understanding what the results are likely to be. Their mental gyrations can be exhausting, and they sometimes fear the fact that there are at least two distinct people inside of them. Their partner must be comfortable with this and, ideally, loves them for it.

# Undying Love

Geminis can be cynics, so when they find a soul mate, they are both elated and amazed. Geminis are smart and worldly, but thinking about the latest facts and the perfect comeback line can keep them from hearing their heart speak to them. Geminis need to understand that love is one area of life where analytical intelligence isn't a help. In fact, it can be something of a hindrance.

Geminis don't expect to be disappointed in love, but rather they find it hard to believe that such a perfect understanding can exist between two people.

# Expectations in Love

Communication excites Geminis, while silence and detachment turn them off. They interpret silence as a form of opposition and feel that they are being ignored. Geminis do not have just two or three opinions to express; it is as though they are two or three different people, and this characteristic must be accepted by those who want to be close to them. Their changeability can be annoying or interesting. The degree to which a Gemini is overwhelmed by confusing emotions will determine how warm or cool, or close or distant, he appears to be.

While Geminis feel emotions deeply, they find it difficult to express love. They need to see that their personal freedom and personal space are being respected. Knowing that they can become too emotionally dependent on another person worries them. They are very sensitive to their own hurt feelings. Choosing words carefully and making sure to be understood are very important in a relationship with a Gemini. Two people can hear the same words but interpret them in radically different ways.

# What Geminis Look For

Geminis need to connect with other people, though they need not be nearby physically. Connecting to others through books, films, instructional videos, as well as through lectures and live performances, is what interests Geminis. They need the freedom to explore, investigate, and learn. Frequent opportunities to change direction, and follow several lines of interest at once, are essential. Geminis are not intellectual snobs and do not require a love interest who is highly educated—only someone who is curious about and excited by ideas.

# If Geminis Only Knew...

If Geminis only knew that it is just as easy to become the story as it is to repeat it, they would avoid gossip, even though it intrigues them. Stretching or elaborating the truth is not uncommon for Geminis, as they can hardly resist embellishing a story. Most people want to be known for their unwavering commitment to a bunch of opinions about what is true about life—most people other than Geminis, that is. With their remarkably adaptable nature, Geminis thrive on new ideas and opinions and are generally open to a change in perspective.

# Marriage

Geminis will be drawn to a special someone who will stimulate them with brilliant concepts and ideas and who will enjoy people and friends as much as they do. They need a stimulating social life, so it is never wise for them to marry a wallflower.

The person who contemplates marrying a typical Gemini must realize that his mate has probably already had more than one partner and will not stay long with a person who is a stick-in-the-mud. Geminis are so mercurial that they need a partner who is willing to move, travel, and change plans often—or else the relationship won't work.

Geminis can be more high-strung than almost any other sign, but we like to say that you have to be high-strung to make great music together.

# Gemini's Opposite Sign

Sagittarius is Gemini's opposite sign. Sagittarius can show Gemini how to look past her own Mercury-ruled fascination with details in order to see the broader view. Sagittarius has a great sense of humor, but unlike that of Gemini, it does not revolve around witty comments or wry observations. Sagittarius knows how to make fun of himself. Both signs are keen on education, conversation, and most of all, ideas. Like Gemini, Sagittarius needs a relationship that is based on far more than simply superficial attraction or sexual desire.

# Pairing Up

*In general, if people display the characteristics typical of their sign, intimate relationships between a Gemini and another individual can be described as follows:*

## Gemini with Gemini

Harmonious, with amazing conversation as a highlight

## Gemini with Cancer

Harmonious, if Cancer is willing to listen to what Gemini has to say

## Gemini with Leo

Harmonious in public, less satisfying in private

## Gemini with Virgo
Difficult, because too many details dominate

## Gemini with Libra
Harmonious—a true mutual admiration filled with affection

## Gemini with Scorpio
Turbulent and emotional, but a real love match

## Gemini with Sagittarius
Difficult, but with a potential for teamwork

## Gemini with Capricorn
Turbulent, especially if values are different

### Gemini with Aquarius

Harmonious—a true meeting of the minds!

### Gemini with Pisces

Difficult, because Pisces wants to lean on Gemini

### Gemini with Aries

Harmonious, with special emphasis on passion and shared goals

### Gemini with Taurus

Harmonious, so long as there are shared goals

# If Things Don't Work Out

Because she loves to be free without question, a Gemini does not feel comfortable with a partner who is harsh, jealous, or dominating. Confinement and boredom are the worst horrors to a Gemini; if a relationship ends, one or both of these elements is likely the culprit. There are rarely any bad feelings on Gemini's part—only a sense of wistfulness for what has been lost.

# Gemini at Work

If a Gemini's work is boring or not challenging enough for his skill level, the best way for him to deal with it is to stay at his present job while planning and taking action to change jobs, or even careers. The time Geminis spend daydreaming about a new line of work might actually help them find a way to improve the experience of their present job—and they might even find that changing jobs is unnecessary. It might also be beneficial for Geminis to hold more than one job at a time. This will bring them into contact with more people who are in a position to help them.

A Gemini should let her desires be known in a way that conveys to others how they can benefit by helping the Gemini. The art of politics is first making the right connections and then using those connections skillfully.

If a Gemini's work is satisfying, then he may want to start branching out or taking on a second job. Holding two jobs might be easier and more beneficial than holding only one. The Gemini may want to go to school or take on-the-job training, since the chance to study something new is usually highly appealing to those born under the sign of the Twins.

Geminis' career goals or ambitions are rarely realized overnight. They would do best to try to accomplish many small successes over a period of time rather than one or two big ones that require too much pressure or ambition.

# Typical Occupations

The best chance for a Gemini to attain success would be in writing, journalism, lecturing, touring, driving, local travel, or working with her hands. Geminis might be able to craft ways to use their everyday routines to their advantage: clever thinking may help them discover opportunities for improvement in ordinary aspects of modern life.

Working in sales is ideal for Geminis because of their abilities to persuade and talk about anything. No matter what profession Geminis enter, they should learn or craft new techniques to streamline their work and make sure that the path to their career goals is clear. They should take time to study as much as they can about their job and where they want to go with it in the future.

# Details, Details

Taking things a step at a time and paying attention to every detail are paramount to a Gemini's success. Making lists and establishing plans to accomplish goals in a logical order are very important to a Gemini. Details are not at all boring; rather, Geminis consider details the essence of their relationships with others as well as the embodiment of their job. This preoccupation with the particulars doesn't mean that a Gemini can't see the larger view of things. She understands that the larger picture is made up of a million little details.

Geminis see all sides of a situation, which can create the impression that they're not committed to anything. They may also appear to be nosey, while, in fact, they are simply collecting details of office life and occasionally talking about them. There is nothing malicious, though, in the way they talk about others.

## Behavior and Abilities at Work

*In the workplace, a typical Gemini:*

* is invariably an "idea" person
* is not always punctual
* can be a problem solver
* has creative ideas
* is well liked by colleagues

# Gemini As Employer

*A typical Gemini boss:*

* is good at charming his employees

* is open to new ideas that will increase profits and cut costs

* makes changes to improve communications

* possesses an interest in the smallest details

* is approachable

* knows how every department works

* socializes with her employees

# Gemini As Employee

*A typical Gemini employee:*

* likes a lot of activity

* enjoys running errands to get out of the routine

* likes to work on several projects at the same time

* can come up with a good idea quickly

* gets bored with bureaucratic red tape

* possesses an aptitude for multitasking

# Gemini As Coworker

Geminis are good at small talk and office politics. They can keep a secret only if they can share it with at least one person, any person, anywhere in the world. Skilled at communication, they can help facilitate interactions between people who are not as good at expressing themselves. They enjoy being editors and fact checkers, and if you have a puzzle that needs solving, ask a Gemini. They are also fun, entertaining, and easy to work with.

# Money

Building wealth is a game requiring discipline and the realization that small things matter. It would be helpful for a Gemini to learn all she can about accumulating and managing money—by reading books, taking courses, and so forth. Asking a successful relative for advice about how to attain and manage financial goals would also be beneficial. Then, whatever a Gemini learns should become a part of her everyday routine.

Investments related to communications, publishing, transportation, or education can benefit Geminis. Whatever they invest in, they should get out and see for themselves what the company really does and how it all works. Simply understanding an investment from an analytical point of view won't be enough.

## At Home

As they are in the workplace, Geminis are perpetually in motion at home. They love having friends over for meals and are the most likely of all the twelve signs to work from their home.

Geminis hate the very possibility that they will be bored, so it is not uncommon to find them making several rooms in their home do double duty. Unlike most signs, they are quite happy to have their bedroom or kitchen be their office, their living room, or their game room; it keeps them from wasting time going from room to room.

## Behavior and Abilities at Home

*Gemini generally:*

* likes a space that is light and cheery

* decorates with a variety of colors and interesting artwork

* needs a big bookcase

* likes to entertain

* enjoys making crafts for her home

* has lots of games to play

## Leisure Interests

Typical Geminis like to listen to the television while they read, or have music on while they sing along and do the dishes. They need to be involved with a lot of activities to occupy their busy minds. They enjoy a good conversation or writing funny e-mails. Geminis often keep a diary, with some maintaining a continuous series of them dating back to childhood.

*The typical Gemini enjoys the following pastimes:*

- reading books and newspapers
- playing table tennis and billiards
- going bowling
- learning and using languages
- creating handmade gifts
- traveling short distances
- watching reality and variety shows
- taking short courses about new subjects
- testing interesting recipes

## Gemini Likes

* telling a good story
* completing crossword puzzles
* doing several things at once
* planning trips
* talking on the phone
* heat-and-serve food or takeout
* being with friends
* novelty gifts
* gossip columns
* knowing a little about a lot of topics

# Gemini Dislikes

- losing an argument
- waiting for an answer
- wasting time
- committing to a date
- inflexible people
- listening to complaints
- not knowing what's going on
- dealing with slow thinkers
- having to repress an opinion
- boredom and boring people

# The Secret Side of Gemini

Because they are good at so many things, Geminis may give the impression of knowing everything. They are restless, and people who are just getting to know them may think that Geminis flit around from one passion to another too often. But it's not so much that Geminis change their mind a lot; rather, it's as though each Gemini individual is made up of several different people. By being of many minds at the same time, they remind us that there is not just a single way to look at a person or a problem.

# Mercury ☿

In Roman mythology Mercury is the messenger of the gods. The modern associations of the planet bearing the same name include all forms of communications, such as speech, writing, sign language, body language, facial expressions, and code. The planet also rules the means for such communications, such as writing implements, books, telephones, computers, wireless devices, pagers, televisions, satellites, and radios. Additionally, it rules puzzles, gossip, and mental activity.

Mercury is the planet of thought and ideas.

Communication often requires an individual to move to different locations, so Gemini is associated with travel undertaken with a practical purpose in mind. It is the sign of busyness, taking care of the routine matters that are the necessities of life.

# Bringing Up a Young Gemini

A parent should use fanciful and imaginative ways to get on a Gemini child's wavelength. Any kind of personal contact through words, ideas, gossip, or philosophy is a lifeline to a Gemini and turns a little tyke into a happy, inspiring, and devoted person. Geminis love it when they are given a lot of attention, and they enjoy learning about almost any subject.

Young Geminis should be taught how to distinguish between illusion and reality since they tend to live in a world where imagination and actuality are so mixed together that it is hard for them to determine where one ends and the other begins. These children will enjoy learning to communicate, read, and speak several languages. In fact, they can easily become multilingual if spoken to in different languages from an early age.

Teaching a Gemini child to slow down a little can be difficult, but it will help her blossom into a more focused adult. Geminis tend to skim the surface and may avoid finishing a chore or an assignment simply because they have moved on to the next thing that has piqued their interest.

More than anything, Gemini children need to be understood. They are naturally honest and will avoid telling the truth only as a defense mechanism when they feel misunderstood.

# Gemini As a Parent

- is able to tune in to a child's world
- encourages creative expression
- is not a strict disciplinarian
- has a sense of humor
- promotes educational goals
- sets high standards
- is considered "cool" by her children's friends

# The Gemini Child

*The typical Gemini child:*

- is happy, bright, and alert
- may have trouble falling asleep
- usually learns to read quickly
- is extremely talkative
- can be quite adventurous
- will become cranky if tired
- moves quickly
- may be a tattler

- loves singing and gabbing
- needs lots of toys and games
- is friendly to adults
- is good with his hands
- sometimes has an imaginary friend

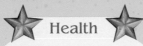

## Health

Geminis need to be careful of problems such as asthma, bronchitis, and the flu. This is because they tend to be nervous types who keep going even when over-tired. They can become very run down, and their resistance is affected if they don't get enough rest. But they hate to be confined to bed! They sometimes have a problem taking good care of themselves because they are constantly on the go and often forget to adhere to regular eating and sleeping schedules. They must therefore try to establish a healthy routine and balance, which will reduce their erratic energy levels. Gemini "rules" the arms, hands, and shoulders; care must be taken when lifting weights or rushing to accomplish a chore.

# FAMOUS GEMINIS

Mary Cassatt

Joan Collins

Bob Dylan

Clint Eastwood

Ralph Waldo Emerson

Michael J. Fox

Judy Garland

Bob Hope

Angelina Jolie

John F. Kennedy

Nicole Kidman

Cyndi Lauper

Tara Lipinski

Marilyn Monroe

**Mary-Kate and Ashley Olsen**

Cole Porter

**Joan Rivers**

Maurice Sendak

**Brooke Shields**

Donald Trump

**Queen Victoria**

Walt Whitman

**Gene Wilder**

Venus Williams

**Frank Lloyd Wright**

# About the Authors

Internationally known self-help author Monte Farber's inspiring guidance and empathic insights impact everyone he encounters. Amy Zerner's exquisite one-of-a-kind spiritual couture creations and collaged fabric paintings exude her profound intuition and deep connection with archetypal stories and healing energies. Together, they have built The Enchanted World of Amy Zerner and Monte Farber: books, card decks, and

oracles that have helped millions discover their own spiritual paths.

Their best-selling titles include The Chakra Meditation Kit, The Enchanted Tarot, The Instant Tarot Reader, The Psychic Circle, Karma Cards, The Truth Fairy, The Healing Deck, True Love Tarot, Animal Powers Meditation Kit, The Breathe Easy Deck, The Pathfinder Psychic Talking Board, and Gifts of the Goddess Affirmation Cards.

For further information, please visit: **www.TheEnchantedWorld.com**